Andrew Woods

OXFORD GRAMMAR 1

Name: _____

Class: _____

OXFORD
UNIVERSITY PRESS
AUSTRALIA & NEW ZEALAND

CONTENTS

OXFORD UNIVERSITY PRESS

TOPIC 1: NOUNS

UNIT 1.1 — What is a noun?

The name game

1 Draw lines to match each picture with a name.

book

dog

sun

box

pin

bag

tap

shop

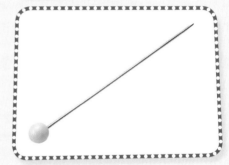

OXFORD UNIVERSITY PRESS

Some words name things.

2 Circle the best naming word.

dig   dog

cup   sip

bag   carry

ship   shut

tree   try

ball   kick

fox   fix

flap   flag

NOW TRY THIS!

Draw pictures and write the names of five things you could see on a farm.

The Monsters' pets

Here are the Monsters.

Here are the Monsters' pets.

Sami

Em

ant

dog

Trang

Cara

duck

cat

Ali

Max

spider

pony

Some words name things.
Legs, **wings**, **pets**, **bag**, **cup** and **car** are all names of things.

Read with your teacher.

1 Draw lines on page 6 to match the Monsters' names with their pets.

  a Trang likes pets with six legs.

  b Sami likes pets with wings.

  c Ali likes pets with eight legs.

  d Max likes pets that say "Meow!"

  e Em likes a pet that she can ride on.

  f Cara likes pets that can bark.

> The words we use for people, places and things are naming words.

2 Which naming words can be pets? Tick.

  a puppy ___   **b** hill ___   **c** bird ___

  d cup ___   **e** shop ___   **f** bag ___

  g rabbit ___   **h** mouse ___   **i** kitten ___

  j fish ___   **k** water ___   **l** door ___

  m lizard ___   **n** key ___   **o** car ___

  p apple ___   **q** lock ___   **r** horse ___

  s lamb ___   **t** jelly ___

NOW TRY THIS!

Can you write the names of three more animals that can be pets?

_____

The Monsters at the beach

Naming words are used for people, places, animals and things.
Naming words are called nouns.

Look at the picture of the Monsters at the beach.

1 Tick the nouns (naming words) that you can see in the picture.

a girl	_____	**b** house	_____	**c** crab	_____
d baker	_____	**e** sand	_____	**f** horse	_____
g hat	_____	**h** jetty	_____	**i** frog	_____
j lifesaver	_____	**k** island	_____	**l** ship	_____
m pirate	_____	**n** cubby	_____	**o** fish	_____
p dog	_____	**q** sea	_____	**r** flag	_____
s tree	_____	**t** farmyard	_____	**u** sun	_____
v bat	_____	**w** sky	_____	**x** foot	_____

2 Write four nouns (naming words) for things that you can see in the picture which are not in the list above.

_____   _____

_____   _____

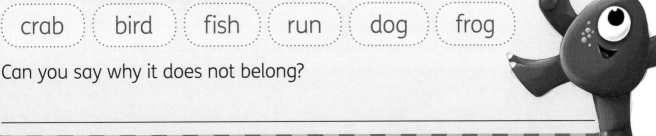

Which word in this list does not belong?

crab   bird   fish   run   dog   frog

Can you say why it does not belong?

_____

Pip and Gog

When there is more than one person, place, animal or thing, the word for it can change.

What differences can you see between the two monsters below?

Here is monster Pip.

Here is monster Gog.

OXFORD UNIVERSITY PRESS

We can **add s** to some naming words to show more than one.
For example: one hat – many hats, one dog – many dogs

1 Add **s** to the naming words to fill the gaps.

   a Pip has one eye but Gog has many _____.

   b Pip has one horn but Gog has nine _____.

   c Pip has one leg but Gog has several _____.

   d Pip has one mouth but Gog has lots of _____.

   e Pip has one arm but Gog has four _____.

2 Make these words more than one by adding **s**.

   a head____   **b** ear____   **c** wing____   **d** toe____

   e finger____   **f** monster____   **g** trunk____   **h** hand____

NOW TRY THIS!

Instead of just adding **s**, there can be other ways to show more than one.
Circle the best answer.

a Pip has one foot and Gog has five (foots / feet).

b Pip has one tooth but Gog has many (tooths / teeth).

c There are five (mans / men) in the team.

d How many (children / childs) are there in your class?

The Monsters' photo album

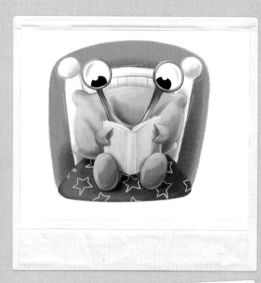

Some words are special names for people. **Cara**, **Max**, **Trang**, **Sami**, **Em** and **Ali** are special names.

1 Write the special names of the Monsters under their photos on page 12.

Cara has a ball.

Max has a book.

Trang has a flower.

Sami has an apple.

Em has a flag.

Ali has a balloon.

> Special names for people, places and things start with a capital letter.

Some words are special names for places. **Melbourne**, **Sydney**, **Australia**, **Queensland** and **Uluru** are special names for places.

2 Add special names to fill in this form about you.

Your first name: _____

Your last name: _____

The name of your town: _____

A friend's name: _____

Your pet's name: _____

NOW TRY THIS!

A boy's name beginning with A: _____

A girl's name beginning with T: _____

A place that begins with S: _____

Monster Town

Here is a map of Monster Town where the Monsters live.

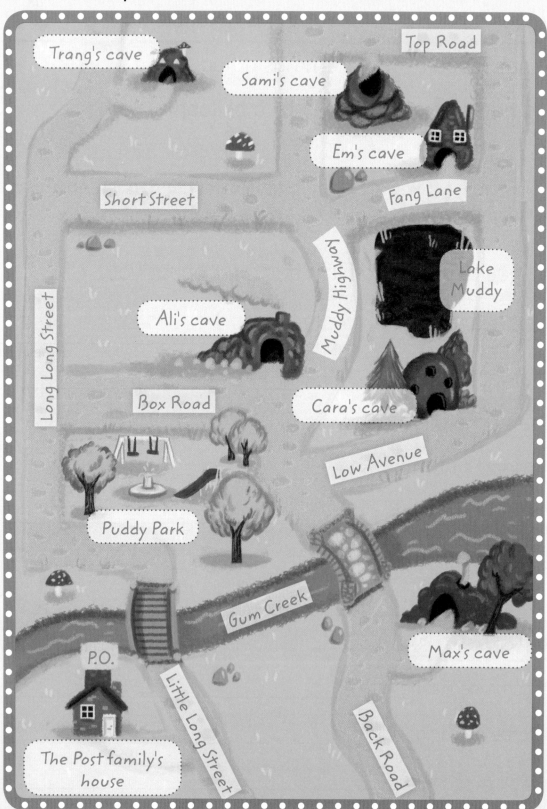

OXFORD UNIVERSITY PRESS

Some words are special names for people and places.
Australia, **Paul**, **Carlo** and **Linh** are special names.

1 Look at the map to see where the Monsters live.

   a Trang lives in _____ Street.

   b Em lives in _____ Lane.

   c Sami lives in _____ Road.

   d Cara lives in _____ Avenue.

   e Ali lives on the corner of _____
      Road and _____ Highway.

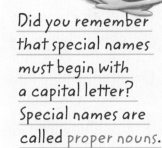

Did you remember that special names must begin with a capital letter? Special names are called proper nouns.

2 Who do you think lives at this address?

6 Back Road
Monster Town
7 0 7 4

_____

3 What is the special name of:

   a Monster Town's lake? _____

   b Monster Town's park? _____

   c the creek? _____

4 On the map, colour the special name of the street where the Post family lives.

NOW TRY THIS!

On the map on page 14 draw and name where the Monster Gang's school could be. Write a special name for the school.

Bip the Bunyip

Read this story with your teacher.

Bip is a bunyip. He lives in Mush Mush Swamp.

Bip's job is to be mean and nasty. For most of the week Bip is very good at his job.

On Monday he scares Tim Taddy.

On Tuesday Bip frightens Danny Duck.

On Wednesday he alarms Magda Moorhen.

On Thursday Bip shocks Pam Possum.

But on Friday when Bip startles himself ...

... he makes Tim, Danny, Magda and Pam laugh all day long on Saturday and Sunday.

OXFORD UNIVERSITY PRESS

1 Use the clues to write proper nouns (special names) from the story about Bip.

The days of the week are proper nouns. They must begin with a capital letter.

   a I am mean and nasty. B_____

   b I am frightened on Tuesday. D_____ D_____

   c Monday is my day to be scared. T_____ T_____

   d I am alarmed on Wednesday. M_____ M_____

   e I am shocked on Thursday. P_____ P_____

   f I am startled on Friday. B_____

2 Where does Bip the Bunyip live? _____

_____

NOW TRY THIS!

Finish these proper nouns for the days of the week.

Monday, T_____ , _____

_____ , _____

_____ , _____

The Monsters play Hidey

Read with your teacher.

We are going to play Hidey.

The Monsters are playing. They are going to play Hide and Seek.

Em, you are IT!

Em is IT. She has to look and chase.

I can see you!

Trang hid behind the flagpole. He got caught.

I can see you!

This hiding place is mine!

Ali hid with Cara. He got caught.

Let's hide here!

I can see you!

Max and Sami hid under a table. They got caught too!

Cara, where are you?

I'm safe at Home!

Cara reached Home. She is the winner.

OXFORD UNIVERSITY PRESS

Instead of naming words, we sometimes use other words for people, places and things. These are called pronouns.

Read the words in this box.

Use words from the box to complete these sentences.

> We I you They
> he she mine

1 The Monsters are going to play a game. _____ are going to play Hidey.

2 Trang hid behind the flagpole but _____ got caught.

3 When Cara asked Max and Sami where they hid,

they said, "_____ hid under a table."

4 When Em saw Ali, she said, "_____ can see you!"

5 When Em could not find Cara, she said, "Cara, where are _____?"

6 Cara said to Ali, "This hiding place is _____!"

We, I, you, they, he, she and mine are other words for people, places and things.

7 Em was IT so _____ had to look and chase.

NOW TRY THIS!

Can you write a sentence with more than one of these words in it?

(we) (I) (you) (they) (he) (she) (mine)

_____

_____

Davy Davy Dumpling

Read with your teacher.

Davy Davy Dumpling

Boil Davy Davy Dumpling in a pot;

Sugar Davy Davy Dumpling and butter
Davy Davy Dumpling;

And eat Davy Davy Dumpling while
Davy Davy Dumpling's hot.

Jack Spratt

Jack Spratt could eat no fat,

His wife could eat no lean;

And so between Jack Spratt and
Jack Spratt's wife both,

Jack Spratt and Jack Spratt's wife
licked the platter clean.

OXFORD UNIVERSITY PRESS

When the poems are read, they do not sound very good because the same nouns (naming words) have been used over and over.

Sometimes, instead of using nouns over and over again, it is better to use other words for people, places and things. These are called pronouns.

Use the short words from the boxes to fill the gaps.

1 Davy Davy Dumpling,

Boil _____ in a pot;

Sugar _____ and butter _____;

And eat _____ while _____ hot.

him
him
he's
him
him

2 Jack Spratt could eat no fat,

His wife could eat no lean;

And so between _____ both

_____ licked the platter clean.

They
them

NOW TRY THIS!

Can you finish these sentences using words from the box?

The book belongs to me. It is _____.

That bag belongs to Jenny. It is _____.

That pen belongs to Dad. It is _____.

hers
mine
his

The Rainbow Snake

(An Aboriginal story)

Read with your teacher.

Long before the First People came to the land, there lived the Rainbow Snake.

To the First People the Rainbow Snake is the father and mother of all life.

The Rainbow Snake has scales on its skin of many colours. They form beautiful patterns.

The Rainbow Snake is so big that as it moves it shapes the land. It forms the mountains and the valleys. It makes long trenches that become the rivers.

When it is tired, the Rainbow Snake crawls into a waterhole and sleeps.

When there is a heavy thunderstorm, the Rainbow Snake wakes up. It comes out of the waterhole. It arches its back across the sky as it looks for a new waterhole to sleep in.

OXFORD UNIVERSITY PRESS

Do you remember?
Nouns are used to name people, places and things.

1 Use the clues to help you finish these nouns from the story.

a f_____ (dad)

b m_____ (mum)

c w_____ (a wet place)

d s_____ (it covers the body)

2 Add **s** to make these story words more than one (plural nouns).

a valley___   b river___   c mountain___

d colour___   e pattern___   f thunderstorm___

3 Proper nouns begin with a capital letter.
Re-write these proper nouns from the story correctly.

a rainbow snake _____

b first people _____

4 Re-write this sentence by changing the repeated proper nouns to pronouns. Use the story to help you.
The Rainbow Snake is so big that as the Rainbow Snake moves the Rainbow Snake shapes the land.

_____

_____

_____

TOPIC 1: TEST YOURSELF!

Nouns, proper nouns and pronouns

1 Shade the bubble below the noun (naming word).

pink   boy   has   can't

○   ○   ○   ○

2 Shade the bubble below the noun (naming word) that matches this picture.

fly   dive   bird   flap

○   ○   ○   ○

3 Shade the bubble below the proper noun (special name) for a person.

rose   Rose   rows   roes

○   ○   ○   ○

4 Shade the bubble below the other word (or pronoun) for **Jack** that could be used to fill the gap.

Jack wanted to visit Monster Town._____took a map with him.

She   They   He   We

○   ○   ○   ○

5 Look at the pictures then finish the sentences using words from the box.

He   mine   you   We   She

a _____ are the

Monster Gang.

b This is Max.

_____ likes to

read.

c Here is Em. _____

has a flag. "This flag is

_____," says Em.

d "I can see _____

behind the tree," said Trang.

HOW AM I DOING?

Colour the boxes if you understand.

Nouns are naming words. ☐

Proper nouns are special names. ☐

We, I, you, they, he, she, mine are pronouns (other words for

people or things). ☐

OXFORD UNIVERSITY PRESS

TOPIC 2: ADJECTIVES

UNIT 2.1 — Some words tell us about other words

The race

Ready, set, GO!

START

A **slow** car

An **old** car

A **sleepy** car

A **fast** car

A **broken** car

FINISH

Who do you think won the race?

_____

OXFORD UNIVERSITY PRESS

Some words tell us more about nouns.

a **big** tree, a **green** leaf, a **pretty** flower

Big, **green** and **pretty** tell us more about a tree, a leaf and a flower.

1 Write the car number.

a Ali has a **slow** car. _____

b Trang's car is **fast**. _____

c Em has an **old** car. _____

d Max's car is **broken**. _____

e Cara has a **sleepy** car. _____

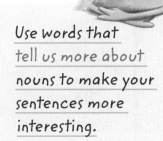

Use words that tell us more about nouns to make your sentences more interesting.

2 Write the five words from above that tell us more about the cars.

_____

_____

3 Some words can tell us more about the cars in the race. Fill in the blanks with the correct colour.

a Ali has a _____ car.   b Trang has a _____ car.

c Em has a _____ car.   d Max has a _____ car.

e Cara has a _____ car.

NOW TRY THIS!

On a separate piece of paper, write some words that tell us more about what these animals are like.

a a tiger   b an elephant   c a shark

Monster mates

Tam has a **tall**, **thin**, **pink** pet.

Pat has a **big**, **fat**, **yellow** pot.

Dot is a **sad**, **sick**, **blue** monster.

Mot is a **slow**, **sleepy**, **purple** monster.

Tom has a **long**, **angry**, **red** face.

Mit is a **wet**, **sloppy**, **green** monster.

OXFORD UNIVERSITY PRESS

Some words tell us more about (describe) other words.
a **red** car, a **clever** student, a **little** cat, a **round** house, **seven** children
Red, **clever**, **little**, **round** and **seven** describe the car, the student, the cat, the house and the children.

1 Write the words that tell us more about:

a Tam's pet   t_____ t_____ p_____

b Pat's pot   b_____ f_____ y_____

c Dot the monster   s_____ s_____ b_____

d Mot the monster   s_____ s_____ p_____

e Mit the monster   w_____ s_____ g_____

f Tom's face   l_____ a_____ r_____

2 Colour Tam's tall, thin pet.

Colour Pat's big, fat pot.

Colour sad and sick Dot.

Colour slow and sleepy Mot.

Colour wet and sloppy Mit.

Colour Tom's long, angry face.

Words that tell us more about (describe) naming words are called adjectives.

Circle the words in this sentence that describe the monster.
The huge monster was grey and hairy.

Ali's cubby

Ali is making a cubby. First he hammers some strong, thick beams.

On the beams, Ali nails long, flat boards for the walls.

Next Ali puts down a smooth, wooden floor.

Then he cuts out a small, square window.

When he has finished, Ali sits in a soft chair.

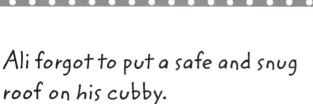

But here come some big, black clouds and ...

Ali forgot to put a safe and snug roof on his cubby.

OXFORD UNIVERSITY PRESS

1 Read the story about Ali. Add adjectives (describing words) to finish these sentences.

   a The beams in Ali's cubby are s_____

   and t_____ .

   b The walls are made of l_____ , f_____ boards.

   c The floor is s_____ and w_____ .

   d The window is s_____ and s_____ .

   e Ali's chair is s_____ .

   f The clouds are b_____ and b_____ .

   g The roof should be s_____ and s_____ .

2 On a separate piece of paper, draw a **wet**, **cold** and **sad** Ali.

NOW TRY THIS!

Write adjectives that describe these faces.

_____ _____ _____ _____

Chinese New Year

Read with your teacher.

It is time to celebrate!

There will be:

- colourful costumes
- dazzling fireworks to scare away bad luck
- loud music and lively dances
- busy markets selling yummy food
- glowing lanterns.

There may be red envelopes with money inside for lucky children.

There will be a grand parade with a fierce but friendly dragon to bring good luck.

OXFORD UNIVERSITY PRESS

1 Use the story to help you write the correct adjective.

a The costumes will be c_____.

b The fireworks will be d_____.

c The food will be y_____.

d There may be r_____ envelopes with money.

e The children will be l_____.

2 Draw lines to match the adjectives (describing words) with the words they tell us more about.

glowing	parade
busy	lanterns
grand	markets
lively	music
loud	dances

Adjectives are describing words.

3 Which two words in the story describe the parade dragon?

_____   _____

NOW TRY THIS!

Look at the photo on page 32. Can you write adjectives to match these words?

t-shirt _____   teeth _____

pole _____   eyes _____

Adjectives

1 Shade the bubble below the adjective (describing word).

The huge elephant swished her trunk.

  ○   ○   ○   ○

2 Shade the bubble below the adjective (describing word).

The clown gave me a blue balloon.

  ○   ○   ○   ○

3 Shade the bubble below the adjective (describing word).

"Fold the square paper in half," said Mr Dan.

  ○   ○   ○   ○

4 Shade the bubble below the adjective (describing word).

Dad cut the cake into twelve slices.

  ○ ○   ○   ○

5 Read each sentence. Then draw on and colour the clown on this page.

Words that describe the size, shape, colour and number of nouns are called adjectives.

a I have a large, red, floppy hat.

b I have a happy face with a pink nose.

c I have blue hair.

d I have a yellow shirt.

e My pants are purple with green spots.

f I have big, black boots on my feet.

g I am juggling three small, orange balls.

HOW AM I DOING?

Colour the boxes if you understand.

Some words tell us more about other words. ☐

Adjectives tell us more about nouns. ☐

Adjectives are describing words. ☐

UNIT 3.1 — Some words are doing words

Ziggy's robot

When Ziggy tells his robot Benny what to do, Benny does it.

Some words are called doing words because they tell us what is being done.
*I **eat** cake. We **drink** milk. They **lick** their ice creams.*
***Eat, drink** and **lick** tell us what is being done to the cake, milk
and ice creams.*

1 Write six words that tell us what Benny can do.

_____   _____

_____   _____

_____   _____

*Doing words tell us
what actions are
being done.*

2 Tick the things in this list that you can do.

walk ___	run ___	jump ___	climb ___
fly ___	sleep ___	swim ___	skip ___
melt ___	work ___	burst ___	try ___
drive ___	count ___	smile ___	knit ___
cook ___	mow ___	play ___	see ___
sail ___	throw ___	wash ___	wink ___

NOW TRY THIS!

Write what Benny can do.

_____   _____   _____

The Monsters' Sports Day

Here is a picture of the Monsters at their Sports Day.

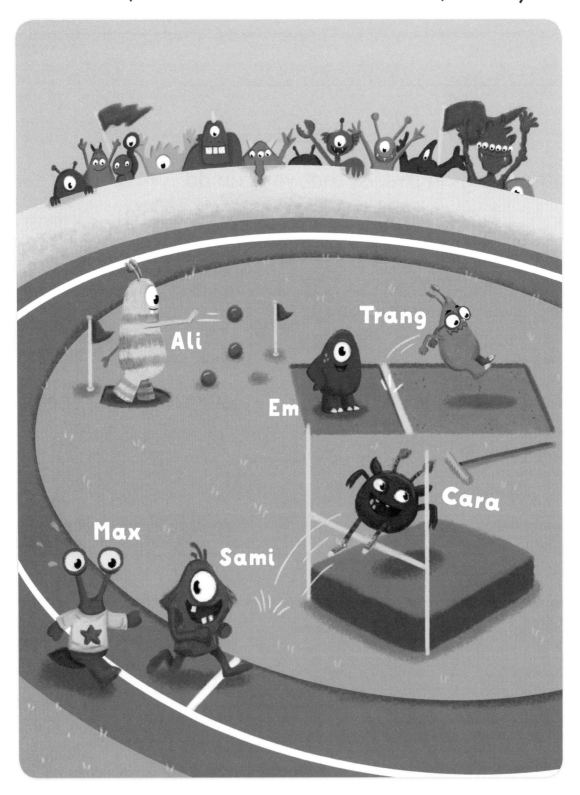

Some words are doing words. They tell us what is being done or what is happening.

Run, **jump**, **win** and **wait** are all doing words.

1 Use the doing words from the box to say what is happening at the Sports Day.

> throwing   waiting   jumping
> running   winning   leaping

Words that tell us what is being done are called action verbs.

a Ali is _____ a shot put.

b Trang is _____ into a sandpit.

c Cara is _____ over a bar.

d Sami and Max are _____.

e Sami is _____ the race with Max.

f Em is _____ for her turn.

2 Match the doing word groups in Box A with the words in Box B.

A
- wash, scrub, dust, sweep
- slide, chase, catch, swing, kick
- cook, fry, boil, stir, eat

B
housework
dinner
playtime

NOW TRY THIS!

Write three doing words telling what you might **do** at the swimming pool.

_____

Pet Day

Do you remember the Monsters' pets?

My pet is called Geeup.

My pet is called Daddles.

My pet is called Tabby.

My pet is called Morton.

My pet is called Octo.

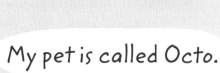

My pet is called Ruff.

Do you remember?
Some words are doing words. They tell us what is being done or what is happening. Doing words are called verbs.

1 Match the names of the pets with verbs they can do.

a I **bark** and **wag** my tail. _____

b I **spin** a web. _____

c I **lick** Max's face. _____

d I **gallop**, **trot** and **canter**. _____

e I **walk** quickly and **feel** with my antenna. _____

f I **fly**, **quack** and **waddle**. _____

2 Write verbs from the box to show how the animals move.

> jump   run   crawl   creep   slide   swim   wriggle
> fly   slither   squirm   leap   flap   flutter

snakes _____   fish _____

worms _____   frogs _____

cats _____   butterflies _____

NOW TRY THIS!

Can you write the names of animals that might make these sounds?

_____s roar, _____s neigh, _____s squawk

_____s hiss, _____s bellow, _____s buzz

Let's make easy naan

Read with your teacher.

Naan is a flatbread that comes from India.

Here is a way to make easy naan.

You will need:

» $1\frac{1}{2}$ cups of plain yoghurt

» 2 tablespoons of oil

» $2\frac{1}{2}$ cups of self-raising flour

What you must do

1 *Mix* together the yoghurt, oil and flour in a bowl to make a dough.

2 *Break* the dough into 16 pieces.

3 *Roll* the pieces into circles.

4 *Press* each piece until it is flat.

5 *Heat* a pan until it is hot.

6 *Toss* the flatbread dough into the pan.

7 *Cook* until the flatbread dough bubbles.

8 *Flip* the flatbread dough.

9 *Cook* until the naan is golden.

10 *Eat* your naan with your favourite sauce or dip.

OXFORD UNIVERSITY PRESS

1 Use verbs from the recipe for easy naan to fill the gaps in these sentences.

a _____ together to make the dough.

b _____ each piece until it is flat.

c _____ a pan until it is hot.

d _____ the flatbread dough into the pan.

e _____ the breads until they are golden.

2 Write verbs from the box to finish these sentences.

> wash   eat   cut   dip

a You can _____ an apple in half with a knife.

b Here is some sauce to _____ your naan into.

c After cooking you should _____ your dishes.

d When you _____ your naan it will taste yummy.

NOW TRY THIS!

Draw lines to match.

eat	flew
feel	ate
fly	felt

Verbs

1 Shade the bubble below the **verb** (doing word).

boy	robot	walk	desk
○	○	○	○

2 Shade the bubble below the word that tells what action is being done in the picture.

fish	swimming	mask	seaweed
○	○	○	○

3 Shade the bubble below the **verb** that finishes the sentence.

Sami _____ to the shop and back.

feet	ran	legs	runned
○	○	○	○

4 Shade the bubble below the **verb** in this sentence.

Ruff barks loudly at the front gate.
    ○ ○   ○ ○

5 Draw and write three actions that you can do with a ball.

_____   _____   _____

6 Draw lines to match these things with what they do.

The wind	flies.
A baby	jumps.
A kangaroo	rings.
A bell	blows.
A runner	nips.
A jet	jogs.
A crab	cries.

HOW AM I DOING?

Colour the boxes if you understand.

Verbs are doing words. ☐

Verbs tell us what has happened, what is happening or
what will happen. ☐

UNIT 4.1 'When' words

When did that happen?

Cara had no hair yesterday.

Today she has some hair.

Tomorrow Cara will have lots of hair!

Sami climbed into a box before.

Sami is hiding in the box now.

Sami will jump out and scare Em and Ali later.

OXFORD UNIVERSITY PRESS

Some words tell us **when** something happened.

Use the page opposite to help you finish these sentences.

1 _____ Cara had no hair.

2 _____ Cara has some hair.

3 Cara will have lots of hair _____ .

4 _____ Sami climbed into the box.

5 _____ Sami is hiding in the box.

6 Sami will jump out and scare Em

and Ali _____ .

Words that tell us when something happened are called adverbs.

NOW TRY THIS!

Finish these sentences about something you have done, something you are doing and something you will do.

Yesterday I _____ .

I am _____ **now.**

I will _____ **later.**

Waiter! Waiter!

Anton the waiter serves food here.

Anton the waiter serves drinks there.

Tabby the cat sleeps here.

Tabby the cat sleeps there.

Sometimes ...

... food and drinks go everywhere!

OXFORD UNIVERSITY PRESS

Some words tell us **where** something happened.

1 Read 'Waiter! Waiter!' Use **where** words from the story to answer these questions.

a Where does Anton serve food? _____

b Where does Anton serve drinks? _____

c Where does Tabby sleep? _____ and

_____

d When Anton trips over Tabby, where does the food and drink go? _____

2 Use **where** words from the box to complete these sentences.

> Words that tell us where something happened are called adverbs.

(inside   outside   up   down)

a The bird flew _____ into the treetops.

b The skateboard rolled _____ the hill.

c When the rain started we ran _____ .

d When the sun came out we walked _____ .

NOW TRY THIS!

Use this **where** word in a sentence of your own:

(backwards) _____

_____

_____

In the jungle

If we creep silently into the jungle and listen and look carefully, we might see and hear a scene like the one in this picture.

OXFORD UNIVERSITY PRESS

Some words tell us how something has happened, is happening or will happen.

Use the picture on page 50 to help you write how words from the box to complete these sentences.

> gently   softly   heavily   quickly
>
> loudly   slowly   noisily   peacefully

1 The snail crawled _____.

2 The lion roared _____.

3 The elephant stomped _____.

4 The bear slept _____.

5 The monkeys chattered _____.

Words that tell us how something happened are called adverbs.

6 The cheetah ran _____.

7 The mouse squeaked _____.

8 The gorilla rocked her baby _____.

NOW TRY THIS!

How must you creep into the jungle to see a scene like the one on page 50?

_____

Phrases

1 Draw:

a Humpty **on the wall**.

b the cow jumping **over the moon**.

c Jack jumping **over the candlestick**.

d Mary's flowers **in a row**.

e the mouse running **up the clock**.

f Old Mother Hubbard going **to the cupboard**.

2 Look at this picture of a playground.

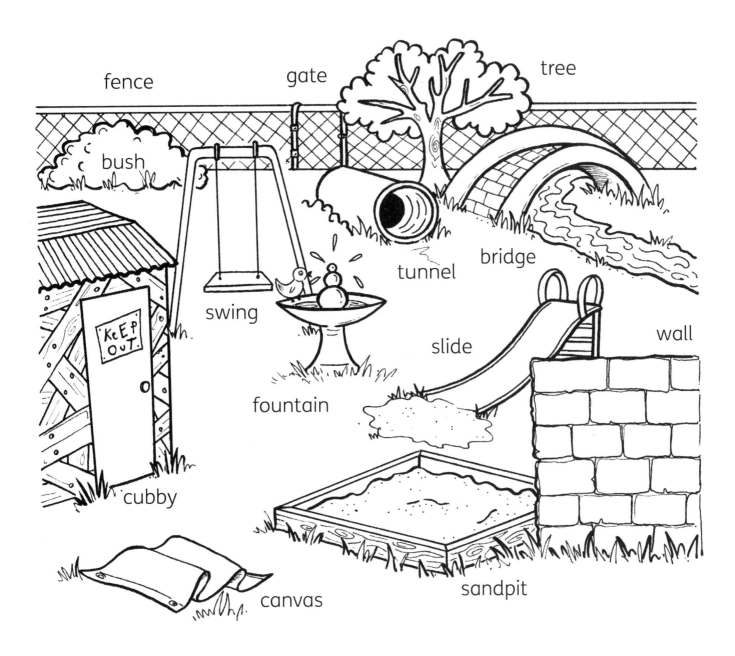

fence   gate   tree

bush

tunnel   bridge

swing   slide   wall

KEEP OUT

fountain

cubby

canvas   sandpit

If the **fountain** is HOME, write some good places to hide in a game of Hidey. Colour in the places you choose.

a in the _____

b behind the _____

c on the _____

d under the _____

e up the _____

f near the _____

Monsters at play

Do you remember the Monsters? Here they are at play.

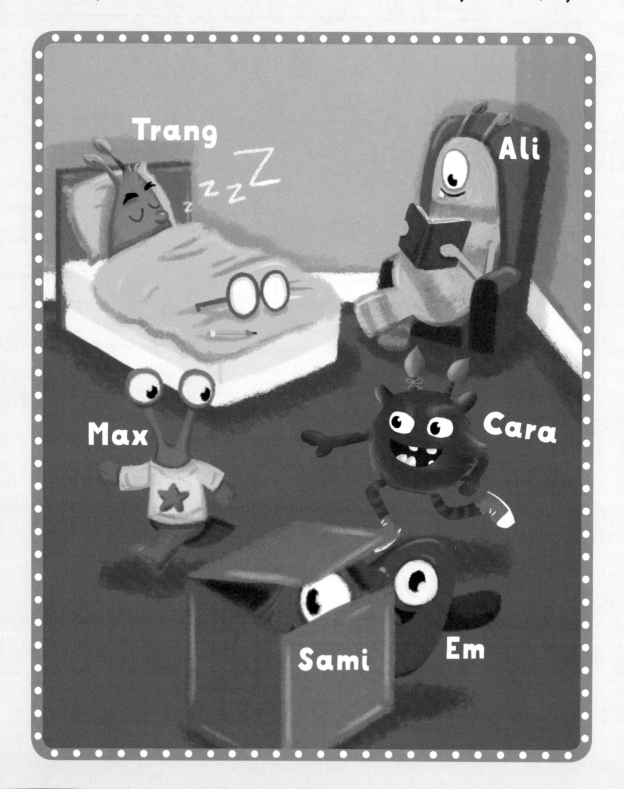

Use adverbs or phrases from the box to finish the sentences about the Monsters at play.

> on a chair   behind the box   quickly
>
> loudly   quietly   inside the box

1 Cara is running _____ to catch Max.

2 Sami is hiding _____.

3 Trang is snoring _____.

4 Em is hiding _____.

5 Ali is sitting _____
_____ reading a book.

NOW TRY THIS!

Write sentences of your own to finish these:

Last week I _____.

Today I _____.

Next year I _____.

Adverbs and phrases telling when, where and how

1 Shade the bubble below the word that tells **when** something happened.

box   some   early   walk

○   ○   ○   ○

2 Shade the bubble below the word that tells **where** something happened.

outside   slowly   today   now

○   ○   ○   ○

3 Shade the bubble below the word that tells **how** something happened.

yesterday   quickly   everywhere   moon

○   ○   ○   ○

4 Write a group of words to tell **where** Cara and Em are in the picture.

Cara and Em are _____.

5 Write adverbs from the box telling when, where or how to finish these sentences about the pictures.

> quickly   far   near
>
> Today   anywhere   hard

a Ali is _____ (where)

    but Sami is _____ (where).

b (When) _____

    it is hot so Max wore a hat.

c Em rode her skateboard _____ (how) past Sami.

d Trang is pushing _____ (how) but the log won't move _____ (where).

HOW AM I DOING?

Colour the boxes if you understand.

Adverbs tell us where, when and how things happen. ☐

Phrases are groups of words that tell us where, when and how things happen. ☐

TOPIC 5: TEXT COHESION AND LANGUAGE DEVICES

UNIT 5.1
Repeating can make understanding easier

Billy's itch

Billy has an itch in the middle of ...

... the pitch!

Billy's itch makes him wiggle and jiggle.

Tilly and Titch giggle to see Billy wiggle in the middle of the pitch.

Milly and Mitch shake their fists at Billy.

SILLY BILLY! You should be in the middle of the GOAL!

OXFORD UNIVERSITY PRESS

Some words are repeated to make understanding easier.

Use the story on page 58 to help you answer these questions.

1 Who is the story mainly about?

_____

2 In the story, how many times has the author repeated:

   a the name *Billy* _____

   b the words *in the middle of the pitch* _____

3 Find two matching rhyming words in the comic strip for each word below.

   a itch _____   _____

   b wiggle _____   _____

   c Billy _____   _____

4 Why wasn't Billy in the goals?

   Because he had an _____

NOW TRY THIS!

Read the story again. Find words that mean the same as these words.

   a laugh _____

   b centre _____

   c playing field _____

Under the sea

Let's dive!
There are jellyfish, catfish,
angelfish and clownfish too!

Here is a beautiful coral reef
with many colourful fish
swimming around it.

Now we have reached the sandy
bottom of the sea.
There goes a crab.
He wants to hide under a rock.

Here comes an octopus with
eight long arms.
We should keep an eye out
for hungry sharks.

It's time to swim back up to the
surface. If we are lucky we might see
a dolphin playing on the wave crests.

OXFORD UNIVERSITY PRESS

Some words **belong together** because they are about the same subject.

1 Where might you see the creatures in the story on page 60?

_____

2 Tick the names of things that best **belong** under the sea.

umbrella ☐	catfish ☐	crab ☐
train ☐	desk ☐	coral reef ☐
shark ☐	whale ☐	sunken ship ☐
seahorse ☐	shell ☐	piano ☐
diver ☐	sand ☐	fruit tree ☐

3 Draw lines to match each group of words with where they best **belong**.

tractor paddock barn hayshed

computer desk locker playground

tie pants skirt scarf coat

gorilla elephant giraffe kangaroo

school

zoo

farm

wardrobe

NOW TRY THIS!

Write the names of some things you might find in a kitchen.

_____

_____

_____

Six silly songs

Humpty Sami sat on a wall
Humpty
Sami had
a great ...

Little Miss Em sat
on a tuffet
Eating her curds
and whey
When down came
a spider
And sat down ...

Ali be nimble,
Ali be quick
Ali jump over the ...

Otto's playing tennis
The sky is blue above.
Olga's playing tennis too
I think the score is ...

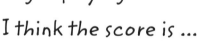

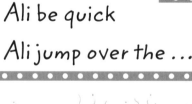

Six swaggering sailors
set sail on stormy seas.
Six seasick sailors said,
"Back to the seashore ...!"

Jojo juggles jam jars,
Juice is juggled by Jess,
Jimbo juggles jelly,
And Jed cleans up the ...!

OXFORD UNIVERSITY PRESS

Some words rhyme.

1 Can you finish the rhymes from page 62?

   a Humpty Sami had a great _____.

   b And sat down _____.

   c Ali jump over the _____.

   d I think the score is _____.

When two or more words in a row begin with the same sound, it is called alliteration (say *uh-lit-er-ay-shun*).

2 Use words from the box to finish these sentences to show alliteration.

> *Rhyme and alliteration are two ways to make poems entertaining.*

| jam | naps | seas | sail |

   a Six sailors set _____ on stormy _____.

   b Jojo juggles _____ jars.

   c Noisy Neddy never _____.

NOW TRY THIS!

Can you finish these tongue twisters that show alliteration?

   a See silly Sally shearing sixty _____.

   b P _____ P _____ picked a peck of pickled peppers.

Text cohesion and language devices

1 Shade the bubble below the word that is repeated in this sentence.

Some frogs live in rivers while other frogs prefer trees.

some	frogs	rivers	trees
○	○	○	○

2 Shade the bubble below the best subject to match the group of words in the box.

dogs	cats	rabbits	birds

people	zoo animals	pets	insects
○	○	○	○

3 Shade the bubble below the word that would best complete this rhyme.

The clock on the wall said half-past eight.

I said to myself, "Oops! Now I'm _____."

nine	weight	wait	late
○	○	○	○

OXFORD UNIVERSITY PRESS

4 Shade the bubble below the word that would best complete this sentence.

Seven silly sausages sailing seven _____.

seas   rivers   creeks   oceans

○   ○   ○   ○

5 Complete this rhyme.

Noisy Neddy never naps.

Noni hogs the nest.

Mucky Marty makes a mess.

Maybe Mummy needs a _____!

6 Complete your own alliteration sentences.

a Finn found five flying f _____.

b Susie saw s _____   s _____.

c Bobby bought b _____   b _____.

HOW AM I DOING?

Colour the boxes if you understand.

Sometimes words are repeated to make understanding easier. □

Some words belong together in groups. □

Some words rhyme. □

UNIT 6.1 — Who? Did what? Where?

The Monsters at the playground

Here is the playground where the Monsters play.

OXFORD UNIVERSITY PRESS

Some words in a sentence tell us who or what the sentence is about.
Some words in a sentence tell us what is happening.
Some words in a sentence tell us where something is happening.

The boy sat on the chair.

Who is the sentence about? **The boy**
What did the boy do? **sat**
Where did the boy sit? **on the chair**

Here are the Monsters.

Em   Max   Sami   Ali   Trang   Cara

A group of words that tells us where is called a phrase.

Draw the Monsters in the playground on page 66.

Who? Is doing what? Where?

1 Sami is playing on the flying fox.

2 Em is hiding in the tunnel.

3 Trang is resting under the monkey bars.

4 Cara is sitting on the swing.

5 Ali is standing near the fountain.

6 Max is playing near the tyres.

NOW TRY THIS!

a Draw yourself in the Monsters' playground using one of these to help you …

near the roundabout	under the flying fox	on top of the tunnel
by a tree	on the monkey bars	between the two trees

b Write a sentence about your picture telling Who? Did what? Where?

The Monsters at home

A sentence is a group of words that makes sense.
A simple sentence tells us one main idea. For example:

Who or what?	Is doing what?	Where?
The dog	is sleeping	under the table.

| Sami | Em | Trang | Cara | Ali | Max |

1 Use the picture on page 68 to help you write six simple sentences.

For example: *Trang is looking through the window.*

a Em is _____ .

b There is _____ .

c _____ .

d _____ .

e _____ .

f _____ .

NOW TRY THIS!

Draw a circle around the group of words that makes a sentence.

Over the road   First you have to   It might rain tomorrow.

On Saturday   The pen is under   Car is

When we grow up

Read with your teacher.

Trang wants to fly into space.

Cara wants to climb mountains.

Em wants to be a movie star.

Ali wants to invent a lollipop machine.

Max wants to sail around the world.

Sami wants to sleep in till late.

OXFORD UNIVERSITY PRESS

A **simple sentence** must make sense so the reader can understand it.

Tick the box next to each **sentence**.

A sentence must make sense.

1 ☐ Trang

☐ Trang wants to fly into space.

☐ in space

☐ to fly

2 ☐ Em is going to be a movie star.

☐ Em movie star

☐ Em going

☐ is going to be

3 ☐ Max sail world will around to

☐ Max will sail around the world.

☐ Max sail

☐ will sail

4 ☐ Sami sleep late

☐ Sami till late

☐ Sami sleep

☐ Sami will sleep in till late.

NOW TRY THIS!

Tick the box next to each **sentence**.

☐ Cara wants to climb up mountains.

☐ Cara wants to climb.

☐ Cara wants

☐ a lollipop machine

☐ Ali will invent a lollipop machine.

☐ Ali invents things.

☐ to climb

☐ when she grows up

☐ will invent

☐ Ali invents a

The Monsters and friends

Max, Cara and Em are best friends.

Bip, Tim, Danny, Magda and Pam live in Mush Mush Swamp.

Sami is reading a book called *Pet Ducks*.

Ali has called his cubby Ali's Pad.

The name of Ziggy's robot is Benny.

Trang and Morton live in Long Long Street.

OXFORD UNIVERSITY PRESS

Sometimes letters need to be written as capitals.

1 Read 'The Monsters and friends'. Circle all the capital letters.

2 Finish writing the alphabet in capital letters.

A	a	B	b	C	c	D	d		e		f
	g		h		i		j		k		l
	m		n		o		p		q		r
	s		t		u		v		w		x
	y		z								

Names begin with capital letters.

3 Write the names of these people, places or things so that there is a capital letter at the start.

Special names of people and places are called proper nouns.

a max, cara, em _____

b mush mush swamp _____

c pet ducks (*a book name*) _____

d ali's pad _____

NOW TRY THIS!

On another piece of paper write the name of:
- one of your friends
- the state where you live
- a favourite book.

The mouse's tail

Read with your teacher.

The cat bit off the mouse's tail.

"Give me back my tail," said the mouse.

"First go to the cow and fetch me some milk," said the cat.

The mouse went to the cow.

"Please give me some milk," said the mouse.

"First go to the farmer and fetch me some hay," said the cow.

The mouse went to the farmer.

"Please give me some hay," said the mouse.

"First go to the butcher and fetch me some meat," said the farmer.

The mouse went to the butcher.

"Please give me some meat," said the mouse.

"First go to the baker and fetch me some bread," said the butcher.

The mouse went to the baker.

"Please give me some bread," said the mouse.

"If you promise not to nibble my cakes, I will give you some bread," said the baker.

"I promise," said the mouse, so the baker gave her some bread.

The mouse gave the butcher the bread.

The butcher gave the mouse some meat.

The mouse gave the farmer the meat.

The farmer gave the mouse some hay.

The mouse gave the cow the hay.

The cow gave the mouse some milk.

The mouse gave the cat the milk.

But the cat could not give the mouse her tail because she had eaten it.

That was the end of the mouse's tail and that is also the end of this tale.

Sentences tell us something.

The car is red.   **My friend is Carla.**   **I am going home now.**

A mark like this . ends a sentence.

The mark is called a full stop.

It tells us that the sentence has ended.

Finish these **sentences** from 'The mouse's tail'.

Circle the **full stop** at the end of each sentence.

A sentence ends with a full stop.

1 The cat bit _____ .

2 The mouse went _____ .

3 _____ to the farmer.

4 The mouse went _____ .

5 _____ to the baker.

6 The mouse gave the butcher _____ .

7 _____ the cow the hay.

NOW TRY THIS!

Finish the **sentences** that answer these questions.

a What happened to the mouse's tail?

The cat _____ .

b Who did the mouse go to for some milk?

The mouse _____ .

Where's my mum?

Read with your teacher.

Lucy has lost her mother.

"Have you seen my mum?" Lucy asked the horse.

"No, I have not seen your mother. Have you asked the duck?" said the horse.

"Have you seen my mum?" Lucy asked the duck.

"Yes, I have seen your mother. She is in the shed," said the duck.

"Why are you in the shed?" Lucy asked her mother.

"It is time to take my wool off," said Lucy's mother.

"Does it hurt?" asked Lucy.

"No. Would you like to be shorn too?"

"No, thank you. I am too busy playing," said Lucy and off she danced into the paddock.

OXFORD UNIVERSITY PRESS

Some sentences ask something.

What is your name? **Where is the cup?** **How are you?**

When can I start? **Is this your bag?**

Sentences that ask something end with this mark: **?**

It is called a question mark. When you see this mark you will know that a question has ended.

1 Finish these questions from the story. Circle the question marks.

a Have you seen _____?

b Why are _____?

c Does _____?

d Would you like _____?

2 How many question marks can you count on the story page opposite? _____

3 Answer these questions.

a How many fingers are on one hand?

_____

A sentence that asks something is called a question.

b Where do you live? _____

_____

c What is your favourite colour? _____

NOW TRY THIS!

Draw lines to match the questions and answers.

Where do you live?   My name is Lucy.

What is your name?   My birthday is on Saturday.

When is your birthday?   I live in Victoria.

Help!

Some sentences are very short. They show feelings or shouting or orders.

Look out!   **Stop that!**   **Hey you!**   **Please let us in!**

Catch this!   **Ouch!**   **I'm over here!**

A mark like this ! is written at the end of a sentence that shows
a feeling, or that someone is shouting or giving an order.

1 Write the missing marks after these sentences.

*Hey! A mark like this !
means that someone
has raised their
voice. It is called an
exclamation mark.*

  a Help   **b** Look out   **c** Oh no

  d Hey, stop that   **e** Eeek   **f** Take aim

2 Choose a word from the box to write what you think is being said.

Help!

Goal!

Surprise!

Yikes!

NOW TRY THIS!

Can you read these sentences aloud in three different ways?

  • It's a bee.   • It's a bee!   • It's a bee?

Let's play footy!

These photos will help you answer the questions on the next page.

Photo A: Kiri takes them on!

Photo B: Can Meg break the tackle?

OXFORD UNIVERSITY PRESS

1 Use the boxes to help you re-write each sentence correctly.

a (K P .)   photo A shows kiri running with the ball

_____

_____

b (K W ?)   will kiri kick the footy

_____

_____

c (K G . !)   "go kiri" they shouted

_____

_____

d (M ! O .)   "oh no" meg is going to be tackled

_____

_____

e (S M ? C)   can sally catch meg

_____

_____

NOW TRY THIS!

Write your own question for each answer.

Q _____

A The players in Kiri's team are wearing yellow socks.

Q _____

A She is playing rugby.

Sentences and punctuation

1 Shade the bubble below the word in the sentence that tells who the sentence is about.

Max is playing on the tyres.

Max	playing	on	tyres
○	○	○	○

2 Shade the bubble below the words in the sentence that tell the action being done.

The girl is building a sandcastle at the beach.

girl	is building	a sandcastle	at the beach
○	○	○	○

3 Shade the bubble below the words in the sentence that tell where this happened.

The car stopped suddenly at the traffic lights.

The car	stopped	suddenly	at the traffic lights
○	○	○	○

4 Shade the bubble next to the sentence.

○ The blue balloon   ○ On the hill

○ I went to the shop.   ○ After dinner

OXFORD UNIVERSITY PRESS

5 On the lines, write what you think each Monster is saying.

_____.

_____!

_____?

I am six.

_____

_____.

Berry Surprise!

A summer recipe

Here's a great summer drink that's healthy and easy to make.

What you need:

150 g cranberries

150 g blueberries

75 mL fat-free natural yoghurt

50 g strawberries

150 g raspberries or blackberries

a blender

Here's what to do:

1 Rinse the berries.

2 Remove the stems and leaves from the strawberries.

3 Place the fruit in the blender.

4 Blend for 30 seconds.

5 Add the yoghurt.

6 Blend until smooth.

7 Pour your Berry Surprise Smoothie into a glass and ENJOY!

OXFORD UNIVERSITY PRESS

Recipes usually start by listing the names (nouns) of all the things we need.

1 Read the recipe. Which word in the box would name this group of words?

berries

yoghurt

blender

adjectives
verbs
adverbs
nouns

They are all _____.

Recipes need to be easy to read. They usually include steps in order, with commands telling us what to do. **Add the yoghurt** is a command. It tells us what to do.

2 Read the recipe. Write the first command telling what to do.

_____

3 Write a command to give an order to a classmate.

_____

4 Look at the coloured verbs (doing words) in each step of the recipe. In each command, where is the verb usually placed?

at the start ☐   in the middle ☐   at the end ☐

NOW TRY THIS!

Circle the word groups below that give commands.

in the blender   into a glass   Add the yoghurt.

Here's a great   Rinse the berries.   Easy to make

My dog, Doug

I have a dog
and his name is Doug
and a digging dog is he.

Doug digs down deep
while I'm asleep
for a digging dog is he.

When Dad awakes
to the mess Doug makes
"You're a daggy dog!" says he.

But I love Doug
with the digging bug
and I think that Doug loves me!

AjW

OXFORD UNIVERSITY PRESS

Poems often use playful, rhyming lines or rhyming words. For example, **he** and **me** rhyme.

1 Read 'My dog, Doug'. Use different colours to circle each pair of rhyming words.

2 Circle the words in each group that rhyme.

　a Doug　　　bug　　　dog　　　though　　　slug

　b leap　　　deep　　　sleep　　　green　　　deer

　c train　　　claim　　　name　　　blame　　　time

Alliteration (say *uh-lit-er-ay-shun*) is often used to make poems entertaining. Alliteration uses two or more words in a row beginning with the same sound.

3 Which letter is used at the beginning of a lot of words in the poem about Doug? _____

4 Add the letter **d** to complete this line of alliteration from the poem.

　____oug　　　____igs　　　____own　　　____eep.

Poems sometimes end with an exclamation mark to show feelings.

5 Add exclamation marks (!), where needed, to the sentences.

　You're a daggy dog　　　　　　What are you doing Doug

　Stop that, Doug　　　　　　　Doug loves me

NOW TRY THIS!

Why do you think the poet (Andrew) chose Doug as the special name (proper noun) for a dog that spends a lot of time digging holes?

_____

Yummy food!
Delicious drinks!

Live music

Come and join us at the
FABULOUS

Barton School FAIR

FREE
pony
rides
on the
school
oval!

Are you
brave
enough to
visit the
haunted
house?

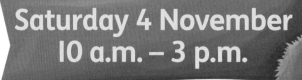

**Saturday 4 November
10 a.m. – 3 p.m.**

Bop the clown will make
an appearance at 1 p.m.

Have fun in the jumping castle!

Lots of amazing stalls and races!

OXFORD UNIVERSITY PRESS

Ads (advertisements) often use exclamations to excite the reader and persuade them to see something or buy something.

1. Read the ad for the Barton School Fair. Circle all the exclamations and exclamation marks (!) used to make the fair sound exciting.

2. Write the question from the ad that asks something about the Barton School Fair.

_____

_____

Nouns (naming words) are found in all texts. The nouns in this text are all about the topic – the Barton School Fair.

3. Add nouns to the labels below to name exciting things you might see at the Barton School Fair. Add some of your own.

castle			

4. Proper nouns (special names) start with a capital letter. Use the clues below to write proper nouns from the poster.

a I am a funny entertainer. _____

b I am the name of the fair. _____

c I am a month. _____

NOW TRY THIS!

Look at the poster and write the adjectives (describing words) that are used to describe these.

_____ drinks _____ stalls _____ pony rides

Opposites

1 Match the opposites. Make each pair of words the same colour.

sad

hot

asleep

out

awake

night

happy

cold

day

in

Some words can have opposite meanings.
Here are some opposites ... **big/small** **fast/slow** **start/finish** **hard/soft**

Finish the sentences.

2 This door is open.

To help you remember, draw pictures that show opposites.

This door is _____.

3 This switch is off.

This switch is _____.

4 This girl is at the top.

This girl is at the _____.

5 This traffic light means stop.

This traffic light means _____.

NOW TRY THIS!

Finish the sentence with opposites.

What goes _____ must come_____.

Words that mean the same

1 Match each group of words that mean the same (or nearly the same) thing by making them the same colour.

happy

wet

sprint

large

little

jolly

big

run

huge

small

damp

soggy

glad

jog

tiny

Some words mean the same or nearly the same as other words.

Put a ring around the word that does not belong in each group.

2

| cup | mug | dish | glass |

3

| hat | boot | cap | helmet |

4

| shed | cabin | hut | swing |

5

| fast | slow | quick | speedy |

NOW TRY THIS!

Circle the word that does not belong.

a   cold   cool   icy   hot

b   little   big   small   tiny

People in the community

I fly an aeroplane every day.

I help people when they are sick.

I fix water pipes when they burst.

I help to keep animals well.

I look after your teeth.

I grow crops for food.

I write books.

I act in films or television shows.

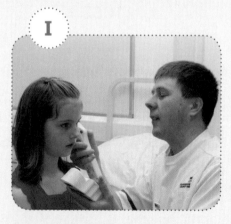

I look after sick people in hospital.

OXFORD UNIVERSITY PRESS

Nouns (naming words) often use **a** or **an** in front of the name: **a** vet
The words **a** and **an** are called articles. We place the article **an** in front
of most nouns that start with a vowel (a, e, i, o, u are vowels): **an actor,
an engine driver, an umpire**

1 Match the job and picture clue with the people on the opposite
page. Write the correct letter in the box.

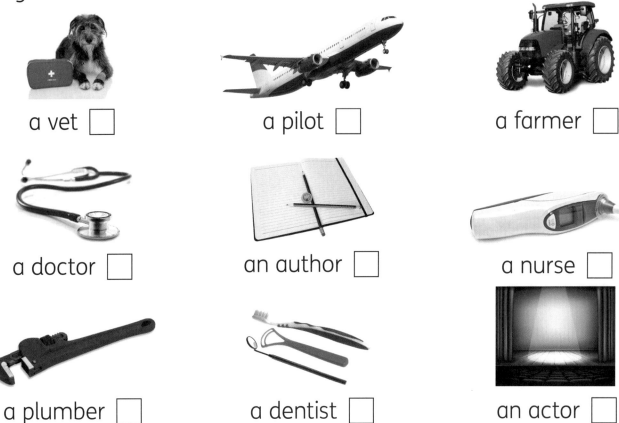

a vet ☐   a pilot ☐   a farmer ☐

a doctor ☐   an author ☐   a nurse ☐

a plumber ☐   a dentist ☐   an actor ☐

2 Circle the articles **a** and **an** in Question 1 above.

3 When do we use the article **an**? _____

_____

NOW TRY THIS!

Name a place where a nurse works. _____

What is something an author might write? _____

Who looks after people's teeth? _____

Spiders

The spider is an arachnid.
Some spiders are dangerous.
A spider is not an insect.
The orb weaver spins a web.

The Sydney funnel-web likes to hide.
The female redback is poisonous.
The female redback has a large, black body.

OXFORD UNIVERSITY PRESS

We can join sentences together by adding **and**, **but** or **so**.

Use the sentences on page 96 and add joining words to make longer, more interesting sentences.

1 _____ and it has eight legs.

2 _____ so it can catch insects.

3 _____ and others are harmless.

4 _____ and she has a red stripe on her back.

5 _____ so shake your shoes before you put them on.

6 _____ but it does like to catch and eat insects.

7 _____ but the male is not dangerous.

NOW TRY THIS!

Using **and**, **but** or **so**, write your own interesting sentence about spiders.

_____

_____

_____

The ant and the grasshopper

Read with your teacher.

It was going to be a long, cold winter.

Ant had been busy. In autumn, he had stored enough food to last until spring.
He had made his little house warm and cosy too.

One very cold winter's evening there was a knock on Ant's front door. It was Grasshopper who was thin and weak from hunger.

"I have not eaten for days and I am cold, weak and hungry," said Grasshopper when Ant opened his door. "Have you any food to spare and perhaps a place by your warm fire?"

"I have heard you chirping away all summer long, Grasshopper," said Ant. "Perhaps your time would have been better spent working rather than singing. You sang all summer and now, for all I care, you can spend the winter dancing!"

And with that Ant slammed his door and left poor Grasshopper to suffer another freezing winter's night.

OXFORD UNIVERSITY PRESS

Some words name people, places and things. They are called nouns.

1 Use nouns from the box to fill the gaps in these sentences.

a It was going to be a long, cold _____.

b Ant opened his _____.

c Ant had made his _____
warm and cosy.

> house
> winter
> door

Some words describe people, places and things. They are called adjectives.

2 Find adjectives in the story that describe the following.

a Ant's house was w_____ and c_____.

b Ant had been very b_____.

c Grasshopper was c_____, w_____
and h_____.

Some words tell us about action. They are called verbs.

3 Use verbs from the box to fill the gaps in these sentences.

a Ant _____ the door shut.

b "You can _____ all winter for
all I care," said Ant.

c "I have heard you _____," said Ant.

> chirping
> dance
> slammed

NOW TRY THIS!

a Find words in the story that mean the opposite to these words.

short _____ hot _____ strong _____

b Find words in the story that mean the same, or nearly
the same, as these words.

skinny _____ small _____ listened _____

Opposites, synonyms and conjunctions

1 Shade the bubble below the word that is opposite to **long**.

high	short	little	heavy
○	○	○	○

2 Shade the bubble below the word that is opposite to **top**.

above	over	bottom	pot
○	○	○	○

3 Shade the bubble below the word that is opposite to **old**.

young	tall	thin	open
○	○	○	○

4 Shade the bubble below the word that means the same as **thin**.

narrow	wide	thick	bad
○	○	○	○

5 Shade the bubble below the word that means the same as **fast**.

slow	quick	small	cry
○	○	○	○

6 Shade the bubble below the word that means the same as **little**.

large	smell	small	big
○	○	○	○

7 Shade the bubble next to the word that would best join the two sentences to make one sentence.

A giraffe is tall. *A meerkat is short.*

○ or ○ but ○ so ○ for

8 Shade the bubble next to the word that would best join the two sentences to make one sentence.

An ant is an insect. *It has six legs.*

○ or ○ but ○ so ○ and

HOW AM I DOING?

Colour the boxes if you understand.

Some words can have opposite meanings. ☐

Some words can have the same or nearly the same meaning. ☐

Some words can be used to join sentence together. ☐

OXFORD UNIVERSITY PRESS

TIME TO REFLECT

Tick each box when you can do the thing listed.

☐ **nouns** I can use naming words when I write sentences.

☐ **proper nouns** When I write the special names for people, places and things, I write them beginning with a capital letter.

☐ **pronouns** I understand that words such as we, I, you, they, he, she and *mine* can be used for people, places and things.

☐ **adjectives** I can use describing words when I write sentences.

☐ **verbs** My sentences always contain a word or words telling what is being done or what is happening.

☐ **when, where and how words (adverbs)** I can use words that tell when, where and how.

☐ **phrases** When I write my sentences, I can use groups of words that tell how, when or where things are happening.

☐ **capital letters** I use a capital letter to begin a sentence.

☐ **full stop** I use a full stop (.) to end a sentence.

☐ **questions** I use a question mark (?) to end a question.

☐ **exclamations** I use an exclamation mark (!) to show that someone is using a raised voice.

☐ **synonyms** I can write words that mean the same or nearly the same.

☐ **antonyms** I can write opposites.

OXFORD UNIVERSITY PRESS

GLOSSARY

adjective	A word that describes or tells us more about other words. *fast, old, black, sleepy, angry*
adverb	A word that tells when, where or how. *today* (when), *here* (where), *quickly* (how)
alliteration	A group of words that begin with or contain the same sound. *seven silly sausages*
antonym	An opposite. *hot/cold, fast/slow, dry/wet, up/down*
article	The words *the, a* and *an*.
capital letter	An upper-case letter. *A B C D E F G H I J K L M N O P Q R S T U V W X Y Z*
exclamation	A sentence that expresses a raised voice or strong feeling. *Stop doing that!*
full stop	The mark (.) that shows us where a sentence ends. *Max is hiding behind a tree.*
noun	A word that names people, places, animals, things or ideas. *girl, ball, beach, forest, table, horse, happiness*
noun group	A group of words built around a main noun. *the long, winding road*
phrase	A group of words that tells us how, when or where. *snoring loudly, it rained today, over the hill, under the bridge*
pronoun	A word that can take the place of people, places or things. *It is Penny's birthday. She is six today.* (he, she, I, it, they, we, us, me)
proper noun	A special naming word for people, places and things. A proper noun always begins with a capital letter. *Cara, Mr Lewis, Australia, Baker Street, Easter*

question	A sentence that asks something. *Are you going to Maddy's party?*
sentence	A group of words, containing a verb, that makes sense. *The birds were sitting on the fence.*
statement	A sentence that states facts or gives opinions. *The horses ran around the paddock.*
synonym	A word that means the same or nearly the same as another word. *cry/weep, run/jog, big/large, unhappy/sad*
verb	A word that tells us what is happening or what is being done in a sentence. Verbs can be: doing verbs: *throw, sit* relating verbs: *am, is, are, was, were, has, have, had* saying verbs: *said, whispered* thinking and feeling verbs: *know, like*

OXFORD UNIVERSITY PRESS